Porcupine

Heather Kissock

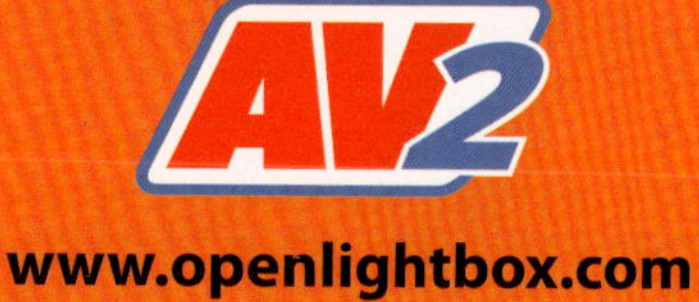

www.openlightbox.com

Step 1
Go to **www.openlightbox.com**

Step 2
Enter this unique code
JFGQSX0QY

Step 3
Explore your interactive eBook!

AV2
Backyard Animals
Porcupine
Start!

AV2 is optimized for use on any device

Your interactive eBook comes with...

Audio
Listen to the entire book read aloud

Videos
Watch informative video clips

Weblinks
Gain additional information for research

Try This!
Complete activities and hands-on experiments

Key Words
Study vocabulary, and complete a matching word activity

Quizzes
Test your knowledge

Slideshows
View images and captions

Share
Share titles within your Learning Management System (LMS) or Library Circulation System

Citation
Create bibliographical references following APA, CMOS, and MLA styles

This title is part of our AV2 digital subscription

1-Year K–5 Subscription
ISBN 978-1-7911-3320-7

Access hundreds of AV2 titles with our digital subscription.
Sign up for a FREE trial at **www.openlightbox/trial**

Porcupine

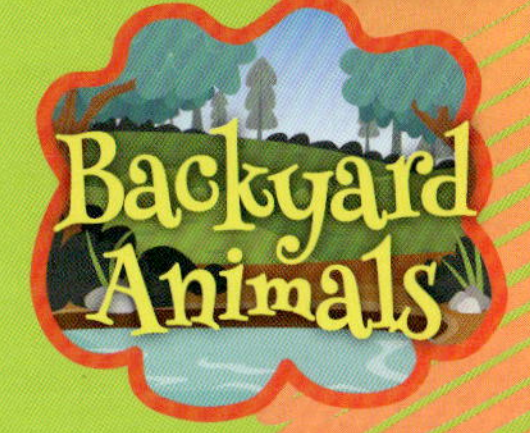

CONTENTS

Meet the porcupine.

He has sharp quills on much of his body.

He lives with his mother when he is young.

When he is young, he learns how to find food.

He is most active at night.

At night, he looks for food to eat.

He eats with his bright orange teeth.

His bright orange teeth help him chew wood and seeds.

He waddles slowly on his strong feet.

His strong feet help him climb trees.

He protects himself with his hollow quills.

His hollow quills help him float in water.

He makes many different sounds to talk.

To talk, he screeches, groans, and grunts.

He likes to live in shady places.

In shady places,
he feels safe.
Porcupine Homes
Caves
Hollow Trees
Snow Banks
Rock Piles

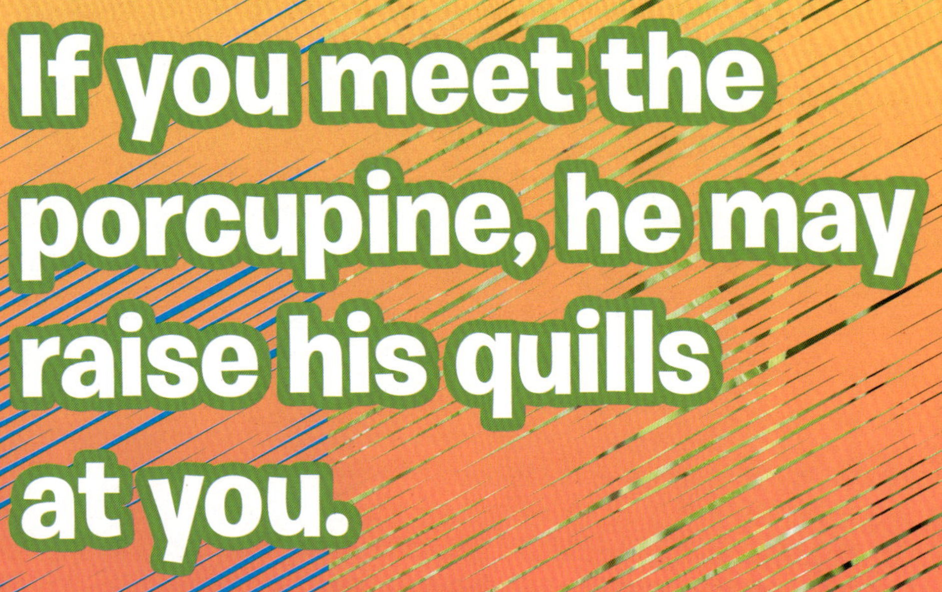

If you meet the porcupine, he may raise his quills at you.

If you meet the porcupine, stay away.

Porcupine Facts

These pages provide more detail about the interesting facts found in the book. They are intended to be used by adults as a learning support to help young readers round out their knowledge of each animal featured in the *Backyard Animals* series.

Pages 4–5

Porcupines have sharp quills. A porcupine is a plump animal with a round head and thick coat. Porcupines are best known for the long, pointed spikes, called quills, growing from their back, sides, and tail. A porcupine can have as many as 30,000 quills.

Pages 6–7

A porcupine lives with its mother when it is young. A female porcupine has only one baby at a time. The baby, or porcupette, drinks milk from its mother. It begins eating plants just a few days after birth. While with its mother, a porcupette learns where to find food and how to protect itself. Porcupettes leave their mothers when they are about 6 months old.

Pages 8–9

Porcupines are most active at night. They are nocturnal animals, meaning they prefer to search for their food in the darkness of night. During daylight hours, porcupines spend most of their time sleeping and can often be seen curled up high in trees. Occasionally, porcupines will also forage for food during the day.

Pages 10–11

Porcupines have bright orange teeth. Porcupines have 20 teeth in total, consisting of 4 incisors and 16 molars. Their teeth are strong, and their incisors never stop growing. The incisors are ground down naturally through the process of eating. Porcupines use their teeth to chew tough wood and seeds.

Pages 12–13

A porcupine has a slow, waddling walk. A porcupine's legs are short, but sturdy. However, the animal has strong feet for climbing trees. The rough soles of a porcupine's feet have no hair, which allows them to firmly grip a tree's trunk. Porcupines may stamp their back feet when they feel threatened.

Pages 14–15

Porcupines use their quills to stay safe from predators. If a porcupine is threatened, muscles in its skin make its quills stand on end. The porcupine can then stick some of its quills into the predator's skin. Although the tips of a porcupine's quills are solid, the shafts are hollow. This helps the animal float in water.

Pages 16–17

Porcupines communicate using a variety of sounds. A female uses high-pitched sounds when trying to attract a mate. Males grunt in response to her call. All porcupines also grunt when searching for food. When a predator comes too close, porcupines chatter their teeth as a warning before using their quills.

Pages 18–19

Most porcupines prefer to live in places that provide good shade. Porcupines set up dens in places that are safe from predators. These include caves, hollow or fallen trees, snow banks, or rocky places. A porcupine's home range typically covers an area of about 25 to 35 acres (10 to 14 hectares).

Pages 20–21

Porcupine quills can cause injury. Porcupines are not aggressive animals. They will try to move away from a threat before using their quills. However, if porcupine quills become lodged in other animals, including humans and their pets, they can gradually move through the body to major organs, causing infection or serious injury.

KEY WORDS

Research has shown that as much as 65 percent of all written material published in English is made up of 300 words. These 300 words cannot be taught using pictures or learned by sounding them out. They must be recognized by sight. This book contains 44 common sight words to help young readers improve their reading fluency and comprehension. This book also teaches young readers several important content words. These words are paired with pictures to aid in learning and improve understanding.

Page	Sight Words First Appearance
4	has, he, his, much, of, on, the
7	find, food, how, is, learns, lives, mother, to, when, with, young
8	at, leaves, most, night, tree
9	eat, for, looks
11	and, help, him
12	feet
15	in, water
16	different, makes, many, sounds, talk
18	likes, places
19	homes
20	away, if, may, you

Page	Content Words First Appearance
4	body, porcupine, quills
8	bark, berries, flowers, grass, nuts, seeds
10	teeth
11	wood
18	caves, rock piles, snow banks

Published by Lightbox Learning Inc.
276 5th Avenue, Suite 704 #917
New York, NY 10001
Website: www.openlightbox.com

Library of Congress Control Number: 2022947017

ISBN 978-1-7911-4482-1 (hardcover)
ISBN 978-1-7911-4483-8 (softcover)
ISBN 978-1-7911-4484-5 (multi-user eBook)

Printed in Guangzhou, China
1 2 3 4 5 6 7 8 9 0 26 25 24 23 22

102022
100921

Project Coordinator: Heather Kissock **Art Director:** Terry Paulhus

The publisher acknowledges Alamy, Minden Pictures, Shutterstock, and Dreamstime as the primary image suppliers for this title.